Climbing the Ladder

To Love

By

Marla D. Jackson

ISBN: 1-4107-2248-1 (e-book)
ISBN: 1-4107-2249-X (Paperback)

This book is printed on acid free paper.

1stBooks - rev. 04/08/03

Ruby was different. She realized at an early age that she was different because she always wanted different things out of life from her friends. They all wanted to marry the football stars and go off somewhere and live happily ever after. Ruby just wanted to have fun and be free. Ruby was from a small town in Florida where her mother was a homemaker and her father was a Holy Ghost preacher who lived by the bible to every word.

Ruby was a very sheltered child. When she was growing up, she went to school and church and had no social life so she made her own social life when her parents were not around. The sad part was she had a twin brother, Randall, who because he was a boy could do anything he wanted to do, which led her to do what she wanted to do. The first time she had sex was one time she had beat her brother home from school and this boy in her class said he always wanted her, and at that time that was all she needed to hear so she laid down and let him have her. It hurt so badly that he had to mistake her screaming for moaning. After this ordeal, Ruby decided not to have sex again, but that crusade didn't last long. The sad part is she didn't really like him, but she wanted to have sex so that she could say she had sex. At this age, Ruby just knew that she was having fun that was until she found herself 17 about to graduate from high school pregnant. Ruby's parents always thought she was a good girl because all her dirty work was done undercover so how could she tell them that their angel was pregnant. She didn't know how to tell them so she didn't. Months and months passed and she was getting bigger and bigger, so she decided to wear a girdle and carried on her normal activities. When you come from a small town, there are no secrets and it got out soon that Ruby was pregnant but she denied until she had her son, Daniel, seven months later. Having a child changed the way Ruby felt about life and especially her life. Toward the end of the pregnancy, her mother found out because she became very sick. After thinking she was going to die from childbirth, Ruby started connecting to God and asking him for the first time in her life for help. Ruby made it through and she and the baby were okay. She was so horrified that she wanted to get away and by the grace of God, her mother said she would keep her son while she went off to school. So when her son was three months old, she left home and went to school in Texas. Ruby felt she needed this therapy to find out what she wanted in life.

Leaving home was definitely therapy because when she got to school, she saw and did things she never thought she would see and do.

Chapter 1

When young girls leave home and go off to school, their first instinct is to do whatever their parents always told them not to do. Ruby had never felt so free in her life so she wanted to take advantage of the freedom. Ruby was at Texas A & M majoring in English and she was partying and having a good time. She partied herself right out of school. She flunked out of college her first quarter in school and couldn't tell her parents because she was ashamed, so she worked and partied until it was time for her to come back to school. She was

1

having so much fun partying that she was not excited that Texas A & M had let her back in but for the purpose of her parents and her child, she went back. She knew she had to learn how to party and do her work. Soon partying was boring so she began to search for a man to take up her time. Then one day out of the clear, she met Kevin at work. He was younger than she was but he knew everything to say and she knew how to receive it. They had so much fun and for the first time since she had a job that she looked forward to everyday. Here she was a freshman in college, and he was a senior in high school. But she didn't care because he made her feel good.

"You are so beautiful," he said.

Ruby didn't respond because she was not interested at first. But Kevin was persistent and he knew he had to come at her like an adult.

"Can I take you out sometime?"

Ruby continued to ignore him but everyday he would ask her the same questions.

"Okay, she said, "Let's go out so I can see if you can back up all this talk."

Kevin was so excited that Ruby had given him a chance that he went and bought a brand new outfit. Although Ruby said she didn't like him, she was intrigued by how smooth his talk was and she was interested in seeing what he had to offer.

The night of their date, Kevin arrived around 7:30. They had plans to go the movie and to go out to dinner. They left and went to the movies and had a great time. When they got to dinner, they engaged in some deep conversation.

"I feel in love with you the minute you walked in the room" Kevin told her.

"I have never seen anyone as beautiful as you are and I want you to be my girl."

"You seem to be a very nice young man, but you are younger than me," Ruby told him.

"The point is do you like me," Kevin asked. I do like you but-"There is no but, Kevin interrupted, then we are going to start dating," Kevin said. They began to spend a lot of time together and they became very close. One night as they were watching a movie, Kevin got very close to Ruby and began to whisper in her ear.

"I love being with you," he said.

"Oh Kevin, I really like being with you," she said. "I'm ready to show you how much I love you," Kevin said.

"I'm ready for you to show me," Ruby replied. Kevin began to kiss her passionately like she had never been kissed before. Her body began to ache for his every touch and he touched her everywhere. He began gently kissing her neck and a chill went

5

over her body and he responded to her body movements.

"I want you so badly," he whispered.

"Take me like you want me," she told him. He kissed her from head to toe and then he slid inside of her and a tingle came all over her body. The lovemaking lasted for about 45 minutes and it was the best 45 minutes of Ruby's sexual experience. He knew how to move with her body and how to make her feel like she was exploding inside.

"Baby, I have never been with someone who made me feel as good as you do," Kevin said.

"Words cannot explain how I feel right now," Ruby, whispered. They were both so exhausted that they laid there naked holding each other for the rest of the night. It was something about the touch of his hand that would glide all over Ruby's body that when she saw him, the hairs on her body would stand in attention. Besides the lovemaking, Kevin was still a child and he was very jealous. Sometimes he would see Ruby talking to somebody else and hate and anger would build on his face. He could get so mad at nothing. Ruby contributed that to his youth but sometimes they would get into heated arguments about nothing and in the end have heated, passionate sex. It was the sex that made Ruby think that it was worth the fighting. His parents felt that she was the best thing that happened

7

to him and at that moment, she felt he was the best thing that happened to her. He graduated and wanted to move away but Ruby didn't want to lose him so she tried to talk him out of it, but he promised her that they would always be together. As she was taking him to the bus station, she cried all the way because it hurt so badly to be losing her man.

"It's going to be alright," he said.

"We are still going to be in touch and I will come back to get you," he promised. Ruby was so emotional that she could not speak. As he got on the bus, he gave her a good-bye kiss and it was so good she just started crying harder. On the ride back, memories of all the time they had spent together kept racing in her head and she pulled over and had a good cry. She cried because she was lonely, because she was alone, and because she was in love. After a couple of weeks of mourning and moping, she got back on the right track and starting living again. They called and wrote each other. After a while, the letters stopped and so did the calling. Ruby assumed he met somebody else and she realized she wasn't in love as she thought so she began to put her life together.

Sometimes after dating someone a long period of time, you don't know what to do when you don't have anybody. That's how Ruby was, she was lonely because she needed somebody so she got back into the party thing and started hanging out but for the remainder of the year, she didn't have a boyfriend and her grades really did improve-she made the Dean's List. By the second year, she was really into passing her classes and had no focus on guys and dating. That was until she met David who was actually one of her best friend's boyfriend but there was something about him.

At first, she suppressed what she felt because she didn't want to lose her friend, Carol, and well he never said anything to her in that way. He was always playing and joking with her, which made her feel good. He was tall, dark and handsome. He had the prettiest dark skin she had ever seen. It almost looked liked velvet. He had the prettiest hair but it didn't matter because he was her friend's boyfriend. Well, one night out the blue, he asked her to go for a ride.

"I need you, he said.

"For what?" Ruby asked.

"Just come with me and I'll explain later," he said.

After getting in the car, Ruby found out that he wanted her to go and stake out his girlfriend's house to see whom she came home with. Ruby was so scared because she knew that her friend Carol was with her lover. They parked across the street from her house for about an hour.

"So, have you talked to Carol today?" David asked.

"No, she said, "I haven't talked to her in a couple of days." Ruby was lying but she didn't know what else to say. They talked and talked until this car rode up and to his disbelief she got out with another guy. He was so hurt but tried to play it off. Ruby knew what was going on all the time but she didn't think Carol would come home that night.

Ruby took him back to her house because he said he wanted to talk.

"I can't believe this bitch is trying to play me," he screamed.

"How could she do this to me?" he asked. Ruby didn't know what to say so she just listened.

"I am going to show that bitch something," he said. He picked up the phone but slammed it down.

"She's not even worth it, to hell with her," he shouted. Ruby could see the hurt in his eyes although he was trying to cover it up. She walked over to him and held out her hand. He held her hand and a warm feeling went over her body. He pulled in closer to her and kissed her and it was a kiss like no other. They stood in the living room just kissing what seemed like for hours. He then took her hand

13

and led her into the bedroom. Her friend's face ran across her mind as he unbuttoned her blouse but the force standing before her was much stronger. He gently unbuttoned each button and took off her blouse as he gazed at her as if she was the only woman in the world. He kissed her around her neck as if it was a piece of dripping, wet fruit. He gently licked her nipples while they stood in attention as if they had never been touched. Her whole body was aching for him this very moment and he took his time and kissed her from her breast to her belly button.

"I need you tonight, Ruby."

"I need you too," Ruby replied. He kissed her like this was going to be his last kiss. She knew when he got to the belly button; he would come back up because every man she had been with had before. Not David, he went down below her belly button kissing her as if he had not eaten a meal in three days. He went inside her vagina with his tongue and she gave a light moan for him to know not to stop. When he came up, he slid inside her as if he had never made love before. He felt so good; Ruby actually felt a tear coming down her cheek. He was moving from left to right, up and down in perfect rhythm with her body movements. As they both felt each other climaxing, they held on to each other as if it were their last time. He looked at her and she looked at him and he just held her for the rest of the night. He felt so good that later that night, they both woke up and repeated the same love making and again climaxing as if it were their last time. The next morning, he had gotten up before her and fixed her breakfast.

"Hey sleepyhead, get up.

"I'm awake but I can't move," Ruby replied.

"Well, you have to because I've fixed you some great breakfast."

Ruby got up and went to put some clothes on but David stopped her and said, "Please don't put your clothes on, you are so beautiful naked. No one had ever told Ruby that and for the first time, she felt

beautiful.

"I know last night was awkward," David told her.

"But I needed you so badly."

I needed you too, but what about Carol?" Ruby

asked.

"I don't know, but I do know we need to talk."

"But I want to see you again and I don't want to

hurt you," he said. "What do you mean?" Ruby

asked.

"I want us to be together but I need to talk to

Carol."

"I agree but you don't need to tell her about us,"

Ruby replied.

"Oh, no! I wouldn't do that baby." It was something about the way he said baby that made her shiver. They agreed that they would talk later and she went to take a shower. As she was showering, David decided to join her. He slid in behind her and began to caress her naked, wet body. Ruby had never done it in a shower and it was so good that tears began to roll down her cheek as they climaxed-again.

Ruby was on cloud nine. It was as if David was still inside her and she had a smile on her face that lit up the whole room. She was so much into another world that she didn't hear the telephone. It was her friend Carol. She was crying and telling Ruby what had happened with David.

"He told me it was over and he never wants to see me again," she whimpered.

"I love him Ruby, why is he doing this?'

"What did he say?" Ruby asked.

"He told me he knew I was cheating on him and he never wants to see me again."

"I begged him to give me another chance, but he just hung up the phone." Ruby couldn't say anything; it was if someone had stuck a knife in her chest. All was running through her head was what had happened with David the night before. She listened as Carol cried and cried in disbelief that she had been caught. She asked Ruby to come and sit with her. As good as Ruby was feeling before the phone call, as she took her shower, it seemed as if her body was in a state of shock. How could she face her friend? Would it show on her face that she had made love to David? What could she do? She knew in her heart that she needed to be there for her friend so she got dressed and went over. As she pulled up, she saw David's car and started to back out when Carol came to the door. Carol met Ruby in the driveway. She asked Carol why was David there.

"He came to ask me why?" Carol said. Ruby and Carol went back into the house and David was pushing 100 questions toward Carol about why and how she could do this.

"As good as I have been to you, how could you betray me like this?" he asked.

Ruby couldn't even look at him so she tried to console Carol. Carol was a nervous wreck and she just cried and cried. Ruby stood there as if she was in another world. David finally just stormed out the door screaming at her that it was over. It was so hard for Ruby to tell Carol it was okay because deep inside she was glad they were not together because she wanted to see David again.

Before Ruby could get home, David had left several messages for her to call him when she got in. He picked up the phone on the first ring.

"I need to see you," he said.

"I need to see you too," Ruby replied. Ruby went to his house and when she stepped into the house, he met her at the door. He threw her against the door and began madly kissing her. He ripped her blouse off and began to caress her breast with a rough but gentle touch. It felt so good that Ruby just moaned and moaned as he went down and gave her the best oral sex she had ever had. Ruby had never climaxed the way she did right there at the front door. But that wasn't the end; he took her in the foyer and made love to her like a man who had been away from a woman in twenty years. When it was over, all of Ruby's clothes had been ripped and she had to borrow his robe to wear home. Ruby was in heaven. She and David were together. They went out to eat, to the movies, and even parties. He would call and she would come running. Carol never suspected a thing and that made it more exciting for Ruby and she was falling in love. The affair went on for over a year and then it was time for David to graduate. The night before graduation, David took Ruby to a nearby beach.

"I am going to miss you so badly," he said.

"I am going to miss you even more," she replied.

"I got this job in Washington, DC and it's too good to pass up," he said. "I know baby, but I will always be here for you when you need me and maybe sometimes, I can come and visit," she said.

He laid her down and made love to her like it was the last time. He ran his hand all over her body as if this was his first time touching a woman. They had never kissed liked they kissed that night and at the end of the night, David told her she was very special to him and he wanted her to always be in his life. It hurt Ruby so badly that he was leaving that she didn't go to the graduation instead she stayed home and cried. She cried because she missed David, and she cried because she thought she was in love. She moped around for weeks after David left aching to be with him. There were some days that she couldn't even get out of the bed. David called a lot but it wasn't the same and she knew as good-looking as he was, he would not stay single long. David and Ruby stayed in contact and Carol never found out what happened.

Ruby was tired of men leaving her and she was content staying away from them. The pain of a man leaving you especially two men is hard. It makes you feel that you can't love because they are going to all leave you. Ruby spent nights up reminiscing about David and their love affair. The things they did, she never would've thought of doing. He made her a new woman and he taught her so much about how to please a man. She missed him but she knew she had to move on especially after the phone call.

"Hello."

"Hi, it's me baby."

Ruby's body began to shiver.

"I've been thinking about you a lot and I met a lady who reminds me so much of you."

"What?"

"I just know this wouldn't work with us because I am too far away and you're too beautiful to just wait on me."

"I understand David and we will always be friends." Ruby hung up crying. "How could he do this to me." "Why is it every time I fall in love, I get hurt?" "Why?" Ruby cried until she cried herself asleep. She was tired of being hurt and she was really ready to give up on love.

Ruby got a job working as a waitress because it was becoming hard for her parents to support her and her child at home. She hated her job and the people she worked with. That was until she met Wil, who was old enough to be her father, but he always made her smile. He always made work so much fun. One night, he asked Ruby if he could call her, and she was shocked but she gave him the number. He called several days later and they talked for hours.

"You're quite an interesting young lady," he said.

"You're quite an interesting old man," she replied.

"Oh, I like the sense of humor," Wil said.

It was near Christmas and Wil wanted to see her before she went home for the break. Ruby was very undecided about what to do but she gave in. Ruby got up early and began preparing her meal. She fixed a beautiful table with candles and had a bottle of wine. Wil got there about 4 p.m. "Everything smells so good, lets eat," he said. As they ate, they talked and drank wine. They were having a good time. Wil came over to Ruby on the couch and said he had a wonderful time and hoped they could do it again. He kissed her briefly then for a long time. He told her he wanted her. Ruby still had this weakness for men who said they wanted her.

"I can't do this right now," she said.

"I need you to do this because I need you," he said. He pulled her closer to him and began kissing. He then slid his hands into her panties. Ruby's body was so warm that she could feel the heat off his hand.

"Please, let's wait," Ruby shouted. His hand between her legs felt so good that her body was aching to have him. He pulled her panties down and entered her with a thrust that made Ruby moaned in pain but it felt good. He was moving inside of her as if every inch of her was so good, he didn't want to miss one bit. It was good to Ruby too and they climaxed together and fell asleep. Ruby left the next day for two weeks. She thought about Wil but she thought it was something that had just happened and it would not happen again.

When Ruby returned to school, Wil began to think that he was her man and they spent a lot of time together at work and at home. She enjoyed his company and he always knew what to say. After a year of enjoying each other's company, Ruby found out she was pregnant. She was very disappointed, but felt that Wil would really be there for her. By getting pregnant, Ruby found out the inevitable, Wil was married and had been married all the time. She was hurt. It wasn't that she was in love with him but she did enjoy him and she cared about him. How could he do this to her? Ruby cried all that night because not only did she find out he was married but he asked her to get an abortion. She was crushed and didn't know who to talk to. She prayed and asked God to tell her what to do and he gave her the right answers. At this point in Ruby's life, God was all she had to turn to. Nine months later, Ruby gave birth to a beautiful daughter Demi. Wil tried to stick around but he loved his wife and although he told Ruby he loved her, he loved his wife more. It hurt Ruby but she had her daughter and she was okay.

Because of financial reasons, Ruby had to do the inevitable; she moved backed home to Florida with her parents. When a woman leaves home, she doesn't want to come back especially with a child. Well, Ruby came home and for the first and only time in her life she hated men. She hated them for all the hurt she had felt, for all the pain she was still feeling and for all the wrongs in her life caused by men. She was in a shell and didn't know how to come out. She stayed in her room and cared for her children. Late at night, she would stay up and cry all night asking God why was her life in such a mess with these men, and why couldn't she find a good man like some of her friends so that she could be happy. Ruby became a bitch from hell. Nobody could get along with her because she was mad at the world and nobody she ran into had the cure for her madness.

She went back to a local college in Florida determined to finish and she talked to her sister, Kitty, a lot. She became one of Ruby's best friends and closet confidant. For the first time in her life, she could talk to someone and let it all out and she understood.

"You have to put God first and everything will work out for you," Kitty would always tell her.

"Your biggest mistake is that you center your life around a man," she said.

"Center your life around God and everything else will fall into place," Kitty said.

Ruby had to learn that lesson on her own but Kitty was determined to help her learn. Ruby always felt she had to have a man. She had to have a man to be a woman-a full woman. Here she was living a life without a man and she was surviving. Of course, there were nights when her body ached for a man but she learned to suppress it at least for a while.

To escape the need Ruby was having for a man, she became involved in school. She became involved in writing and was asked to go to a writing conference by one of her professors. She went on this trip to Baltimore, Maryland, strictly to present her paper and make professional contacts. The conference was great and everyone enjoyed Ruby's presentation. One night, she took a stroll and met up with one of the other students, Edward, and they walked and talked that whole night.

"I really enjoyed your presentation," he said.

"I really enjoyed yours," she replied. They had a lot of things in common. They were both English majors and they both had a talent of writing. The next night as they lay in his room, he began to caress her and she got that feeling back but it was so

35

different. He had a way of touching her that made her want to make love to him like no other. As he was touching Ruby, she kept thinking about how long it had been and every inch of her body waited in anticipation of his next move. They made love that night and it was beautiful and Ruby felt good. She felt even better because she didn't think she would see him again but she did. For almost a year, they had an affair. Ruby called it an affair because after almost two years of satisfaction and love that she gave him, he came to her and told her he was marrying someone else.

"I do love you but I've had a girlfriend all this time," he said.

"What?" Ruby exclaimed.

"Yeah, well, anyway, she's pregnant and I have to do the right thing," he said.

"So making love and promises to me was also the right thing," she said sarcastically.

"I never meant to hurt you." I love you and I will always love you."

"If I had met you before all of this then things would be different but I have to be responsible," he said.

"Responsible?" Ruby inquired. "Yeah, you were real responsible when you told me I was the only woman in your life and now you're marrying someone else." "Go to hell!"

Ruby was hurt and she was about to cry but she couldn't let him see her like this. She took off running like never before until she came to a wooded area. She sat there in the midst of the wilderness and cried like a baby.

"God, why does this keep happening to me," she cried. "God, Why?" "Why?"

She cried for days because she was so hurt that she had given her heart away and he wanted someone else. It hurt so bad that she wanted to shut away and not live. Ruby didn't understand how he could be with someone else. She had given him everything he told her he needed and wanted. She never understood how men could marry someone that they knew couldn't satisfy them. She just didn't understand. She had never hurt the way she was hurting right then. It hurt so bad that when she thought of him, she cried; when she went to bed she cried. She cried and cried and cried but the hurt was still there.

Ruby didn't know how to get through this, her sister, Kitty, helped her a lot. But what she did learn is that God will talk to you and he will help heal your soul when you think you have no one. One night she went to church and the preacher said, "If you are tired of man hurting you, come to Jesus, he will make it all right." She went up crying almost running to the front. She was asking God, "Please take this pain away and show me a new way." From that night, Ruby learned the importance of knowing God. He didn't immediately take the pain away and she felt the pain for a long time. She would think about it and hurt and cry. She has always cried and always wondered did these men cry. Did they hurt the way she hurt? It is written somewhere that you can't love someone else until you love yourself. Ruby thought she loved herself, but why wasn't she getting love in return? She had to do a lot of soul searching to find the answer. She needed God and only God to help her heal. The problem was she didn't know the first thing to do. She wanted to be like everybody else and have a man in her life so that she could one day have a complete family. She knew what her problem was but solving it was the hard part. She had a problem thinking men were the answer. Ruby knew that within, but how could she solve it? She would tell herself that she was finished with men but that didn't help because in her soul, she felt she needed a man.

It's amazing how women try so hard not to have a man especially after so many have hurt them. Ruby had been wounded and her heart didn't need to take anymore but she still had the desire. In order for her not get attached to anyone, she had a sexual affair with Nathan. Nathan was very interesting. He was tall, dark, and handsome. The only problem

41

was that he was very conceited. He felt everyone wanted him. He owned a mortuary and was very successful but most importantly, he knew how to make Ruby feel good. Remember, Ruby was still in to what made her feel good. The affair went on for a while and she was satisfied because it was just sex. There was nothing else and nothing to worry about as far as her heart was concerned. For the first time in her life, she was not hurting and she was fulfilling her desire. The one thing about Nathan was that he had been full of tricks and he always wanted to try something new. That was not easy to deal with because some stuff he wanted to try, Ruby didn't know anything about it. Ruby wondered again why men who had girlfriends felt the need to have

someone on the side. Nathan had a girlfriend but

was calling her every chance he got. That meant

that his girlfriend didn't give him what he needed,

then what was the point in having her? Ruby just

didn't understand and this was not just with Nathan

but also with most black men. It was evident in the

relationships that Ruby had been in, that black men

had a problem committing to one woman. They

would rather have a showgirl on their side than a

woman who satisfied their needs and wants. Ruby

just didn't get it. Why have girlfriends who can't

supply your needs? Why? This was a question that

haunted Ruby but at the same time, she allowed these men to treat her this way.

Everything must come to an end and Ruby was really tired of Nathan using her. Although she was having a good time, she knew it wasn't going anywhere. Through all of this commotion, she graduated from college and got a job teaching Reading and English. She loved her job and a lot of her hurt and pain was lost in her work. She became very much involved in writing and teaching and tried again to forget men, so Ruby ended it with Nathan and tried to live a man-less life.

Well, without Nathan in her life, Ruby didn't have any sex happening. She was working hard and trying to forget men. That's hard for a woman who

has always felt she needed a man. She wanted time

to heal her soul and find out what was God's plan

for her.

Chapter 2

The healing process is the hardest part because that is the time to come out of denial. It is easier to find someone else's faults, but it is so hard to admit to yourself when you have a problem. Ruby had a problem, which is why she attracted the wrong men. She searched for answers to help her heal.

She read the Bible and of course, every answer she needed was in the Bible. Sometimes it's not what we want to hear but it is there, and it helps heal but sometimes we need someone to talk to. Ruby had no one. She couldn't talk to her mother because her mother was the one and only Mrs. Perfect. She never made mistakes but was easy to point out Ruby's mistakes. For the most part, Ruby blamed her mother for the way she was. Her mother sheltered her so much that to get away from her, she went to men because she needed love. Her mother never sat down and told her she loved her, she just told her what not to do. Ruby was wounded from an early age and the men in her life just pushed the wound in further.

Ruby began to read books by spiritual leaders such as Iylana Vanzant and Juanita Bynum. In a lot of ways, these two women helped Ruby with what she needed to do. The question was could she do it?

She read in a book by Juanita Bynum that, "We must learn to survive the wounds." That's what Ruby needed to do; she needed to survive the wounds. Ruby didn't think that her mother could help her wounds because she didn't know what Ruby was going through. Everything to her mother was black and white and that is not how Ruby's life was. Her mother was so into making sure she chose whom Ruby would date, she never saw the pain Ruby was going through. That was a battle itself for Ruby.

Whoever Ruby liked, her mother hated. She always talked about people and class. What puzzled Ruby was her mother didn't know anything about class so how could she say who was in what class? There were just things that Ruby didn't understand about her mother and she was at a point in her life, she couldn't work on her mother; she had to work on herself. She loved her mother, but she never really understood her mother. Ruby needed to heal and listening to her mother was not a part of the healing process. Again Ruby began to read and search for some answers.

She was doing well as far as sex was concerned. Of course, she thought about it, but she always tried to suppress it one way or another. As time went by, it became harder and harder for her to suppress it and her body would ache for it. She would think about Wil, David, Kevin and even Nathan. There were many nights she would pick up the phone to call Nathan and put it down. It was hard but she knew she had to remain strong. Ruby wanted to heal and she remembered Juanita Bynum saying, "Instead of allowing someone to process us through the healing, we think that time heals." That's what Ruby had lived through all her life thinking that time heals all wounds. Many times, when we wait on time to heal the wounds, the hurt just sinks deeper and as we go through different relationships, the hurt piles on top of each other. Ruby had allowed the hurt to pile up and she was hurting even without the presence of a man.

To have someone to talk to, she started confiding in a woman friend, Alice. They became very close and began to share some very intimate secrets and fantasies. They would go out to lunch and dinner and just hang out. Ruby felt safe with this woman because she was a minister. Not only was she a minister, it seemed as if she understood Ruby. Nobody had ever understood Ruby. Everybody always gave her a hard time, except Kitty, about everything and no one ever listened. Alice listened and it seemed as if she cared.

Months went by and Ruby felt good. She had let go of sex and she had someone she could talk to. She felt really good. One day Alice asked Ruby what was her wildest fantasy and Ruby was caught off her feet but tried to come up with an answer. Ruby had never thought of what was her fantasy because she always tried to please her man but not be pleased. She thought for a minute and could not come up with an answer. Alice said, "Well for the last couple of months my fantasy has been to be with a woman." Ruby was knocked off her feet and could not believe what she was hearing. This was a minister who was talking about her wildest dreams of being with a woman. She could not respond but Alice kept talking about the intimate details of being with a woman.

"I sometime imagine at night touching and caressing a woman and having her do the same to me," she said.

"Sometimes, I even think of you," she continued. Ruby couldn't move. When they hung up the phone, Ruby began to think why did Alice tell her all of this? Why would a woman want to be with another woman was a mystery to Ruby. She thought about her experiences with all the men in her life and could see no point in being with another woman. She thought it was sick but Alice brought it up again two weeks later. Alice and Ruby were riding to a church meeting and Alice began talking about how fond she was of her and how she had enjoyed their time together. "I really like being with you," she said. It's like you satisfy something in my inner soul," she continued. Ruby agreed because she had definitely enjoyed their time together. Alice asked Ruby would she have dinner with her after church. Ruby agreed and after church, they went directly to Alice's house. Alice had everything set and everything looked beautiful. Dinner was great and Ruby was preparing to leave when Alice walked out to the living room naked. Ruby was startled and confused.

"I have been dreaming about you all week and wanting to be next to you for a while," Alice said. Ruby was in a state of shock. She had never looked at another naked woman. She couldn't move but

Alice was walking towards her and when she got

close enough, she began kissing her. Ruby didn't

know what to do and she was devastated and scared.

Every nerve in her body had stopped and she felt as

if she were dead. Alice began to lift her blouse and

search for her breasts. As her hand reached her

breast, Ruby could feel something happening and

but she couldn't move. Alice began stroking her

breasts and caressing as if they were a piece of

delicate material. She began to moan and groan and

then she began to take Ruby's panties off, but Ruby

couldn't move but she could feel Alice's hand

running all over her body. Somehow or someway,

Ruby moved away and ran out of the door without her panties. She could never talk to Alice again and avoided her as much as possible. Alice would call and leave messages but Ruby could never talk to her again.

Ruby was so confused. How could this happen? Here's this lady she had trusted and thought was her friend and she had tried to seduce her. How could that happen? Ruby felt she couldn't trust any man or woman. She began to fall deeper into her work and began writing and editing. She needed to get her mind off of what had happened to her.

Then she met Timothy who had an answer for everything. It was funny to Ruby how when she wasn't looking for anybody, everybody popped up.

Timothy was a lot of fun to talk to but he had one

obstacle, he was married. This was something that

she didn't have the energy or the time for in her life.

She ignored him whenever he would bring up sex

and to be married, he brought it up too many times.

He would constantly complain about what his wife

didn't do. At first Ruby didn't let it bother her

because it sickened her that he could talk about what

his wife didn't do but he still stayed there. One

night after they had left a community meeting

together, his car wouldn't start and he needed a ride

to his brother's house. Ruby took him and he

invited her in to meet his brother. When they got

inside, there was no brother and Ruby immediately knew something else was on his mind. It was his brother's house but he knew his brother was out of town. Ruby was very upset and began fussing at him. He told her he was sorry but he needed to spend some time alone and talk with her.

"I'm really attracted to you and I don't know what to do," he said.

"I lie in bed with my wife and think about you," he continued.

"I can't be hurt right now," Ruby said.

I do like you but it's wrong and I'll end up hurt."

"Please don't do this to me," she said.

"Can I just sit here and hold you," he said.

"Yes, I would really like that," Ruby replied.

They began talking and having fun again and the next thing Ruby knew, Timothy had kissed her. It was a very passionate kiss and Ruby hadn't been with a man in so long, it tasted like sweet strawberries dipped in chocolate. She wanted more and he knew it.

He began kissing her harder and passionately. He started kissing her around her neck and her whole body shivered. It felt good to be next to him and she was now aching for him to have her. He took his time with his tongue and began to touch every inch of her body. He then slid inside of her and made passionately love to her the rest of the night. Ruby never knew how he got away with staying the night and didn't care because she had that feeling again and it felt good.

It was different with Timothy. He seemed to really care about her and he took a lot of time to be with her. She was content being the other woman because he was always there. They still had a good time and they always made love to each other like it was their last time and Ruby was in love again. Now Timothy was a real freak and he wanted to act out all his fantasies with Ruby. She couldn't handle some of his fantasies but agreed one night to do whatever he wanted to do. Timothy told her he wanted her to be with a woman. She said ok as long

60

as she didn't know the woman. She wasn't thinking

about herself.   She was thinking about pleasing

Timothy.   Remember Ruby thought she was in love

and she didn't want to lose Timothy.   That night,

they got a hotel room and waited on the third party.

In the middle of making love, there was a knock on

the door and Timothy assured Ruby it would be all

right.   He went to the door and the lady walked in.

At first Ruby wouldn't look up, but when she did

look up it was Alice. She tried to say something but

couldn't.   Here she was lying in bed naked and

Alice smiling in front of her.   Timothy introduced

them and they began to play. Alice wanted Ruby all

to herself, so she began caressing and kissing her

from head to toe. She then went down and gave her oral sex like no man had ever done before. While Alice worked on Ruby, Timothy worked on Alice and they took turns working on each other. Ruby couldn't talk but she could feel and she didn't want Timothy to know that she knew Alice so she just went with everything. When Alice left, Timothy looked at Ruby and told her he loved her. She felt good because no man had ever told her he loved her it seemed as if he really meant it. Several times, Timothy hooked Alice and Ruby together and outside of the hotel room, Alice and Ruby never spoke a word. Ruby hated doing it but she wanted to please Timothy. She loved him and wanted to keep him. It is amazing how quick someone can think they are in love with somebody when really they are infatuated with lust. Ruby knew she had to get away because Timothy was beginning to ask her about more of his fantasies and it took the beauty of sex away for her. She began to break dates or she wouldn't call, and he would call with an attitude, which would make her so mad. Timothy had begun to think that he could tell Ruby what to do and that she couldn't see anybody else. This was definitely not what Ruby wanted or needed so she told him she had somebody else. At first, he tried to pull the guilt trip and make her feel bad but she felt good and she didn't care about what he felt. He then tried to make it seem like he had given up so much to be with her and this was his repayment. It didn't matter what he said because Ruby knew this was it.

Ruby immediately asked God to forgive her for all the things she had done with Timothy and especially Alice. She asked that he wipe her clean. She felt good about leaving Timothy, but she desperately needed help.

Chapter 3

When a person needs help, the first step is for them to know they need help. Ruby knew she needed help, but she didn't know where to go to get the help. She knew she had a problem with sex and men. Why? She wanted love and she took sex from men who just wanted sex. Ruby was miserable and had no one to go to or talk to for help. She prayed a lot but still had this need. It came to the point that she even begged God to help her. One day she realized that in order to receive help, she had to really want help. Yes, she was tired of the

65

relationships but she always found one good thing from each relationship and that was always sex. So when Ruby would ask God for help, in the back of her mind she really didn't want to give up sex. This was just one part of Ruby's battle.

Somehow or another Ruby began to see Nathan again. She still felt the need to have somebody. She couldn't stand Nathan but they always had good sex so she looked over the rest of his faults. His main fault was that he was so conceited. He always thought he had what every woman wanted. He didn't, but Ruby played the game to have some great sex. She was working and writing and trying to get work publish. On top of that, Ruby was a mother to two children. Being a single parent who worked full-time proved not to be so easy to Ruby but she was determined to take care of her children and she did. Ruby tried to make herself busy by working and parenting but there was always a late night sitting up, she wished she had somebody to hold her tight or to make love to her and really love her.

Time passed on and Nathan and Ruby were still seeing each other sexually. One cold night before Christmas, Ruby had a visitor. It was an old friend of her family's Bobby. She was surprised to see him and was puzzled why he was there, but they had a very enjoyable evening talking to each other.

"It is so good to see you, he said. They talked for hours and he told her he would call her later. She thought later meant the next day but he called her later that night and again they talked for hours. "You have really grown up," he said.

"Well, I couldn't stay a little girl forever," she responded. "Yeah, but you are so beautiful," Bobby replied. Ruby was so embarrassed that she couldn't even look at Bobby; she just held her head down. It was amazing to Ruby how they talked as if they had known each other forever. Somehow the conversation sparked to sex and one thing led to another and Bobby was back at Ruby's house. Bobby had been a childhood fantasy of Ruby's. She had admired him for years but as time grew so did

she, and her crushes disappeared. That night, Ruby

became interested in Bobby again and she could tell

that he was interested in her. They had a wonderful

night together without having sex. She lay in his

arms as if his were the only arms to lie in and slept

like an angel. Bobby was in town only for a week

and they spent everyday together or on the phone.

When Bobby left to go back to Georgia, he would

call Ruby and they would talk for hours. Whenever

he would come home, he would stop by and see her,

and they would have great sex. It went on for a

while until Ruby distanced herself from him and

began seeing Nathan again. For some reason,

Nathan was always there waiting on her and she always went back to him.

Ruby felt her feelings for Bobby getting too deep and she wasn't sure what his motives were for the relationship. The one thing Ruby couldn't stand to happen was to get her heart broken again. Bobby would still call and she would talk to him but she was so afraid of getting hurt that she tried to keep her feelings out of it. One night, Bobby called and asked if he could see her. They met at a restaurant and he told her he was considering moving back home. Ruby didn't really get excited but was glad she would have someone to talk to because they did have great conversations. He told her that he had a room and if she would come and spend some time with him.

"Bobby, I'm scared."

"I know, but I will never hurt you," he said.

Ruby believed him and went back to his motel room. They both wanted each other, and it was evident on their faces. Ruby walked into the motel room and immediately headed for the shower. Ruby was surprised that Bobby walked in behind her. He undressed her, and she undressed him, and they stepped into the steamy, hot water, and he took the bath cloth and gently wiped every inch of her body. She could feel the tingle in her body and it felt good. He then gave her the cloth as she gently wiped every

Marla D. Jackson

inch of his body. He then turned her around and gently inserted his penis inside her from behind. It felt so good Ruby was about to scream from pleasure. As he grinded, she rolled her hips and they both climaxed simultaneously. It was beautiful but that wasn't the end. They came to the bed as he passionately kissed every inch of her still wet body. He then slid inside of her, and it felt like no other man she had ever been with. He was a very kind and gentle lover, and Ruby had never been with anyone like that before. He was so passionate. He knew how and where to kiss her that made her want to give him whatever he wanted. What Ruby liked the most was the way he took his time as if he would not be able to make love again. Ruby felt so good, she felt tears coming down her cheeks. Although, it was one of the best nights of lovemaking for Ruby, she was determined not to let her feelings go wild.

Ruby felt good and she wondered where Bobby had been all her life. She was in a good mood for days and Bobby and her met up for several days over the next couple of weeks. Bobby decided a month later to go back to Georgia but promised Ruby he would keep in touch. This was good for Ruby and they talked a lot over the next couple of months. Ruby was glad that she had not fallen in love because she knew then she would not be able to accept him leaving but she was satisfied with the conversation. When Bobby would come home on the weekend, Ruby would see him and they would have a good time. As time passed by, the calling and the seeing of each other seemed to stop so she went back to Nathan. Remember Nathan was always there and he was always willing.

Ruby began to concentrate on being a serious working mother. Ruby would work, come home, play with the kids and go to bed. When that urge would hit her, she would call Nathan. She was content. During this time, Ruby didn't even think about making a commitment or dating someone seriously, she was satisfied or at least she told herself, she was satisfied with the current situations.

A year later, Bobby called Ruby.

"I need to see you," he said.

"For what?" she asked.

"I need to explain to you what happened," he said.

"I don't want to know," she said.

"Please, baby, let me see you."

"Okay, but in a public place."

"I will be home next weekend and I will call you," Bobby said. The next weekend arrived and they went out to eat.

"I know you are wondering what happened to me," Bobby said.

Ruby didn't respond because she didn't know how to respond.

"I was falling in love with you and I couldn't handle it then, but now I am ready to be with you the way I need to be," he continued.

"Do you think that you can just run over someone and just pop up when you get ready," Ruby asked.

"No, I just needed space."

"Then you should have talked it over with me and not just ran away."

"Please give me a chance to make this right."

"Yeah, make it right when you get ready.

Ruby didn't know what to do. She knew she wanted to spend time with Bobby, but she didn't know if he was going to hurt her and she couldn't take that right now.

Bobby ended up staying home for over three weeks and he told Ruby that he was considering moving back home, but Ruby didn't take that seriously because to her their relationship was sexual and that was fine. As time went by, and the more they talked, the relationship seemed to grow into something more. They were lovers but somehow had become friends. It felt good to Ruby to have someone to talk to and make love to in the same night. This had never happened to her before and she felt pretty good.

Ruby was in a good mood. She thought she had found the man of her dreams and he was available- well so she thought.

After Ruby was on cloud nine for about three months, Bobby said he needed to talk to her. He gave this sad story about their age difference and the problems she would have with her family if they continued on with the relationship. Bobby was 20 years older than Ruby, which never seemed to matter when they were making love. And then he told her about Amy back in Georgia whom he had been seeing for over three years. Ruby's heart stopped beating. She was hurt, and she wanted to scream. As tears rolled down her cheeks, she could not say a word. How could he forget to mention that he had someone? How could he take her through all this and have all her feelings involved and not tell her he had someone else? How could he do this? She was so crushed that her body could not move-she was numb from head to toe as he sat there talking about that this was just the wrong place and the wrong time for their relationship.

"It's not that I don't love you," he said.

"It's just that I can't give you what you need," he continued.

"When did you decide that you didn't have what I needed," Ruby asked.

"You came back here saying that you wanted this to work and all of that was a lie," Ruby screamed.

"It wasn't a lie, I did want it to work, but I also love Amy," he said.

"Did you forget to mention Amy when you were begging me to take you back?"

"Please Ruby don't do this," he said. She was so hurt that she wanted to crawl away and die. She was in love with somebody she had a childhood fantasy about, and whom she thought was available. All she could say was, why he didn't he tell her, and he was continuing saying that he did. It hurt more that he didn't even know what he told her. Each conversation would end with Ruby crying and feeling why was this happening?

The sad part about this situation is that Ruby didn't feel that Bobby cared the same about her because how could he hurt her like this? Ruby was terrified because for the first time, she felt she was really in love and that this was the man for her. She couldn't believe all this was happening. After weeks of crying and moping around, Ruby tried to get back to normal but she ate, drank and slept Bobby, and she was hurting. She tried to hate him, but she loved him, and you can't hate someone that you love. For awhile, Bobby and Ruby didn't talk, and when they did see each other they made passionate love and that wasn't what Ruby needed but she wanted him every time she saw him. They told each other that they were just friends, but friends don't have sex. Ruby tried to figure out what her connection to Bobby was because all she knew was that she loved him and she wanted him. Something had to happen but she didn't know what it would take or what to do. She needed to pray because this was bigger than what she could handle.

Chapter 4

Ruby tried not to talk to Bobby, but they would talk every day and she would cry every night because she wanted him, and she wanted to be with him and she wanted him to just want her. He told her that he cared but he couldn't say the words "I love you," but that she should know by how he treated her. Ruby should have left then but she stayed because somewhere in the back of her mind and heart, she felt they would be together. Months went by, and she continued to carry on this affair with Bobby, but she wanted better. In order to do better, Ruby needed to want to do better. Ruby had begun to get back in church, and she was tired of this sin she was carrying on her shoulder. She asked God to help her stop fornicating. And most importantly, she asked him to free her of Bobby. Ruby promised Bobby that they would always be friends, but how was that possible? This man had taken all she had given him and hurt her in the end. How could he do that and how could she allow it to happen? Simple, she thought she was in love.

She tried to be his friend and not his lover, and it took a lot of prayer because he was like the devil. Although he promised that he too wanted a sin-free life, he was always tempting her about sex. It made it hard for her because she always wanted him but she had to take a stand. She prayed and asked God to help her to reject him and to come in and be there for her. She wanted a man to love her for whom she was, a man who wanted to spend the rest of his life with her and most importantly, a man who wouldn't pressure her about sex. She asked God to give her that man and to get Bobby out of her mind. Ruby was in a state where she wanted to get married and settle down and she just didn't see that with Bobby. First of all, Bobby was not financially stable, and he never did anything for her, so how could he provide for her? But Ruby loved him and she wanted to be with him every hour of the day. They would still talk for hours, and yes, they would still meet for sexual encounters and it would be so good that Ruby could not let him go. She felt she needed him, and he took advantage of that need every time he was with Ruby. Ruby believed that he cared and that she wanted, no, she needed to be with someone. Bobby was what she wanted, and she couldn't give up on him because she loved him too much, and she was willing to wait.

The reason Ruby couldn't leave Bobby was because deep down, she really believed that he cared, that it just happened to be the wrong time and the wrong place. She loved him and wanted to be with just him. What Ruby didn't realize is that she had given him everything, and he hadn't given anything. He still had two women. He was allowed to go back and forth, and he didn't see anything wrong with it. He wanted Ruby all to himself, but she didn't have him all to herself. But Ruby was in love, and she couldn't see what he was doing to her, all she knew was that this was the man she wanted to be with the rest of her life.

Time went on, and it delighted Ruby that Bobby was falling in love with her. He looked at her with such love and desire that she looked forward to every time they met. They would meet just to talk, and there would be so much passion that they would end up making endless love all night. Ruby loved this man, and this was her man and no one could take him from her. Time continued on and Ruby and Bobby spent a lot of time together but Ruby was beginning to realize that she needed to make a change and that had to start with herself. Ruby wanted to know what she could do to change so that she could get Bobby out of her life. Oh, yes, she loved him and ached to lie with him every night but in the back of the mind, she knew one day he would wake up and be gone.

Ruby finally moved out of the house with her parents, and that was the perfect opportunity for her and Bobby to have a "real" relationship. He would spend the night almost every night and it wasn't that they had sex all those nights; they just had a good time being together. They would sit up for hours talking and fall asleep in each other's arms. She knew he loved her, so why couldn't he let the other woman go? She wanted to be with just him because he made her so happy.

Time and time went by, and Bobby still carried on the relationship with both women. One day when Ruby got home from work, she looked at her phone bill and noticed that he had been calling the other woman on her phone. She was furious and hurt at the same time. All she could think was that he had no respect or honor for her or her house. She was so hurt that all she could do was cry and ask

God for direction. She knew in her heart that she needed to let him go and she need the strength. She had to prepare for the inevitable. That night, Ruby took her children to her parents and waited for Bobby to come from work. He was late, but that was good for Ruby because she needed that time to regain her strength. She waited and waited and tried to cry all she could because when he got there, she wanted to be ready. He walked in and went straight to the shower, she told him when he finished that she needed to talk to him. As he was taking a shower, he called her into the bathroom to hand him a robe. When she got in the bathroom, he pulled her into the shower. As mad as she was, when she looked at him, she melted. She stood there in the shower as he peeled her clothes off her body and began to kiss and caress her from head to toe. He turned her around and gently entered her from behind. The actual feeling of him entering her made her whole body shiver from excitement. She wanted to give every inch of herself as he was giving to her. He felt good, and she wanted him to feel good. She forgot about the woman, she forgot about the bills, she concentrated on her lover, her man, her best friend.

They made love for over two hours, and all the time that Ruby had known Bobby, he had never been so passionate. It was if he knew what she was about to do that night and he had to stop her. After he went to sleep, Ruby went into the living room and cried and prayed. She knew she still had to let him go. Why was good sex her weak point? What could she do? Bobby missed her in bed and found her in the living room. He wanted to know what was wrong.

"I looked over the phone bill and noticed that you have been calling Amy and I just can't take this anymore," she said.

"I have called her a couple of times, but it was no big deal," he said.

"So it's no big deal that you disrespect me and call some other woman," she asked.

"I love you, so does it matter?"

"Yes, it matters because if you love me, you don't need to call her," she said.

"I'm sorry, baby, but I need you, so let's not make this an issue," he said.

"Let's not make this an issue," Ruby repeated. "You have some nerve," Just go to hell," she screamed as she went to bed. Whenever Ruby tried to let go, he would immediately come with the fact that he needed her and was not ready to let go, but she was unhappy and something had to be done.

So like the fool that Ruby had been, she told him she loved him and would always be there. The problem was that Ruby was miserable with this decision. She couldn't think, eat or sleep because she knew she needed to let him go. She knew she couldn't do it all at once, so she told Bobby that he didn't need to stay every night because it was bad for her children. He understood but Ruby cried every night and she wanted to be with him, but she had to make a stand. Two weeks went by and although they were talking on the phone and had met for lunch, they had not seen each other. Ruby decided to write him a letter explaining to him what she needed and that he was not offering what she needed. She told him he needed to make a choice within the week. He called her furious and told her he couldn't make a choice because he had "invested" all this time with the other woman. Ruby made a stand and told him it was over. She blocked his phone number and wouldn't answer the door when he came. It took her three months to recover but Bobby was out of her life and she could exhale. That was until one day as she was playing with her children in the park, he appeared. He told her he needed to talk to her and would she give him a few minutes. She didn't want to, but she listened. He began to tell her about how he missed seeing her and how he missed talking to her. She wanted to grab him and make endless love to him but she had to be strong. She listened as he talked but all she could hear him saying was that he still wanted her to

95

wait. She knew she couldn't wait any longer so she told him that she would always love him but it had to be over. He said he understood. He kissed her passionately and walked away.

Chapter 5

Ruby still thought about Bobby, and she still missed him. The sad part was that there were still occasions when they would meet and she would drop her eyes. She loved him and probably always would. But through all the crying and staying up at night, she was proud of herself and felt confident about what she had done. She began to work on finishing her degrees and spending time with her children. Her children began to get older and spent a lot of time with school activities, which left Ruby alone. She felt okay because she was sure that when the time was right, she would meet the man she needed to meet.

Ruby finished all her degrees and was doing great financially. She and her children moved from Florida back to Texas. Ruby bought some land in Dallas, Texas, and was beginning to build a house. She was working at a local university teaching literature and she owned a beauty shop. She didn't go the shop a lot but it was good to own something, and the people who worked for her did their jobs. She started to feel good about herself because she was doing some of the things she always wanted to do. Ruby began to realize that one of the reasons she couldn't give as much in a relationship was because she had a lot of growing to do. Once she started growing, she began to love herself and was now ready to give herself to a relationship.

Two years went by and not only had Ruby not had sex, she had not been in a relationship. The good part is that it didn't bother her not to be in a relationship because she was working on herself and it felt good. Ruby's son was preparing to graduate from high school and was going to be attending college in California. Ruby was so proud of him and she knew it would be lonely without him around, but she still had her daughter for another four years and that would be a challenge. Ruby began to see so much of herself in her daughter that she knew she was too hard on her at times. Ruby felt that she had to be hard in order for her daughter not to experience what she had experienced in the past even if that meant sometimes her daughter would have to hate her.

Matter of fact, the day of her son's graduation, her daughter was upset with her but they still had a good family affair. Her son left the next day, and she cried but she knew he had to grow up and become a man. A couple of days after that, Ruby and her daughter went to Florida on vacation to enjoy the last couple of days of summer. Her daughter had a good time and she and Ruby also seemed to begin to bond.

They went to every show, every movie, and every function Florida had to offer. There were some local plays showing and they went to several of the water parks just hanging out and having fun. As they were leaving the movies one night, Ruby heard someone calling her name and when she turned around she was in shock. It was Marcus. Marcus had been in Ruby's life when they were very young. It wasn't even serious enough for her to remember all the details. She remembered that he was 18 and she was 20. She also remembered he left one summer to live in Virginia and she would see him every now and then but that was it. It was good to see him and he looked good. He was a couple of years younger than she was and he couldn't believe her daughter had gotten so grown. They left the movies together to get a bite to eat down the street. As they were eating, some girls came by that Ruby had met on the beach, and she left to go eat with them. This gave Marcus and Ruby a chance to catch up.

"You know, I never forgot you."

"I can't lie, it's been a long time and I had forgotten you," Ruby said.

"Well, back then, we were kids, but if I would have known then what I know now, it would have been different. He told her how much he thought about her and had missed her. He also told her that he had gotten married and was very unhappy. Ruby was so tired of men saying how unhappy they are but still staying in the relationship. She sat there and listened but in her mind she knew that she would not go through this again. They sat there and talked for hours and hours, which was great for her daughter, who was hanging with her friends. All of a sudden Marcus asked for Ruby's number and she looked him in the face and said for what?

"Don't you have a wife?" Ruby was surprised at herself but she gave it to him. He went on to tell her that they were together, but she didn't have what he needed.

"I can't do the things that I use to do," she told him.

"I can't be the other woman for anyone," she said. Marcus told her he understood and that he wanted her to be the woman and that he would return for her. They ended the conversation with the notion that Marcus would be filing for divorce and coming to get her one day, and he hoped she would be ready. Ruby didn't put her hopes too high, and she felt good that it didn't bother her. She was okay with whatever happened. At this point in her life, she just wanted to be a mother to her daughter who was getting to be a handful.

Chapter 6

Two years had passed, and Ruby and her daughter Demi were having a ball. Demi was very active in a lot of sports and activities. This kept Ruby's mind occupied, and she didn't even have the need for a man. Ruby couldn't believe it but it didn't bother her not to have a man. She was content being a full-time mother and teacher. She was now teaching writing courses at a local college and she was negotiating opening a clothing store. She was living out her dreams and she was happy without a man.

One day out of the blue, Marcus called. He was in town and wanted to come by and see her. She agreed to let him come over because Demi was off at cheerleading camp. Marcus came over and was astonished at how beautiful her house was.

"It's like a mansion," he said. It was like a mansion. It was a two-story house with ten bedrooms. It had everything in a house that could be in a house, and Ruby had two expensive cars: A BMW and a Lexus. Marcus could not get over how successful Ruby was, and he was very excited for her. Ruby fixed dinner and they sat out on the patio. Marcus told her when he went back home, he was leaving his wife and he wanted to be with her. For some reason, Ruby felt nothing. She decided just to listen. He went on and on about how he was unhappy and couldn't take it anymore. Again, Ruby had heard it all before. She listened carefully and then he told her how much he wanted her in his life. She could no longer take it so she told him that he was too late because what she once felt, she no longer felt and she was happy being alone. Marcus did not want to hear this so he continued talking trying to convince her, but she wasn't hearing any of it so he gave her his number and left. Ruby was tired and ready to go to bed. She cleaned her kitchen, threw the number away and went to bed.

For the first time, Ruby felt like Ruby and she was so proud of herself.

Around 2 a.m., Ruby's phone rang and it was her son's roommate. He was crying hysterically telling her that her son, Damon, had been in an accident. Her heart fell on the floor, but the roommate was too upset to make any sense so she just got up, threw some clothes in a bag, and got on the first plane to California. She tried to call her son's apartment but could never reach anyone. This made her nervous and upset. When she called the hospital, they couldn't give out information on the phone. After a long flight, she finally arrived in California and went immediately to the hospital. Her son had been in an awful car accident with a drunk driver.

When she arrived at the hospital, she saw her son connected to all types of tubes. He didn't look like himself at all. He was just lying there as if he was already dead. Ruby fell to the floor and began to pray. She was hurting and she immediately began to ask God to step in. "I need my son," was all Ruby could say. For five days, he was in a coma and for five days, Ruby was right there. Her daughter couldn't take it; she would not come into the hospital room because she wanted to remain strong for her mother. One day as Ruby was praying and holding her son's hand, he grabbed her hand. She was ecstatic. She ran to get the doctor, and when she returned, her son's eyes were open. A tear was coming down his face, and he looked as if he had no idea what had happened or where he was. The doctor told Ruby to step outside. She was overwhelmed with joy that her baby was going to make it. Through everything that Ruby had gone through, it was her children that helped her to get through it all. The doctor came out and said all test came back that his mental state was okay and that he looked as if he was going to be okay, but that his speech was slurred, and he had a broken leg. She didn't care what was slurred or broken; she just wanted to see her baby. He was waiting on her, too, as if he was a kid in a candy store. She hugged and hugged him and they talked about the accident. He didn't remember at all what happened. He just remembered being at the library that night. It was late and he was driving back to his apartment. There was a drunk driver swerving in the middle of the road. The drunk driver hit Damon head on and made his car completely run off the road. The drunk driver was killed at the scene. Damon was definitely lucky to be alive. After hundreds of tests were done, Damon was allowed to come home. He went to stay with Ruby and she took care of him. She bathed him, fed him, and drove him to physical therapy. She was glad to take care of him, most importantly, she was glad he was alive. Her daughter, Demi was just as happy. She even stayed home more just to be with her brother. After six months of serious therapy, Damon decided to go back to college. Ruby was so proud of his progress, and even though she would miss him, she was not the kind of mother to hold her son back, so she watched as he drove out the yard and shed her little happy tears. Demi had begun to cheer again and she was gone a lot and Ruby was going back to work.

Ruby realized how much she missed being a parent. She had enjoyed taking care of her son and having her daughter at home. Ruby constantly worried about her daughter because she knew of the pressures in the world for girls. The one thing about Demi was that she seemed to know what she wanted out of life and that was a good feeling for Ruby. Although she felt good rearing her children, she was back to the same old routine and she was lonely. Her job took a lot of her time and when she was home, Demi was usually at some function. The sad part about all of this was that soon Demi would be considering going off to college.

At this point in Ruby's life, she was content not to make the same mistakes but she was weak and right now she needed a man. She was financially stable and she had accomplished everything she wanted out of life. She was successful, but she couldn't make love to her money. She needed to make love and more importantly, she need to be in love.

One day as Ruby was sitting in her office reading essays, one of her co-workers, Fred, came in and asked her to go to lunch. She had been out with him hundreds of times together because they were great friends. They went out and had a couple of drinks and he began to tell her how he was interested in her and wanted to be with her.

"I know this might sound odd, but I really like you," he said.

"No, it doesn't sound odd, I like you too," Ruby responded.

"No, I mean I like you," he said.

Here's the problem: He was married. He told her about the problems he was having and how he wanted to get out. Ruby had heard all of this before and wasn't interested but she was attracted to him. He was a big guy, who was not necessarily Ruby's type, but he was sexy. He had a shiny bald head that made Ruby melt when she would see him down the hall. Anyway, she sat there and listened, but she was really sitting there thinking about getting naked. It had been a long time, and here sat a sexy man who was very much appealing. Ruby finished her drink and told him that they would talk later. On the drive to her shop, Ruby was thinking about Fred

115

although she didn't want to get involved with a married man, it would be less stressful to deal with. The bottom line was that it would end up hurting her more than it would help her, but at this point Ruby needed to be with someone. Ruby had begun to love herself and she was now the person she knew she could be. Still, she had desires and wants, and she wanted Fred.

Whoever said you don't have to have a man was wrong. There are nights when you lie in bed when the only answer is a man. Ruby was tossing and turning, and she was lonely. Demi was spending the night with friends and no one was home to talk to Ruby. Not that Demi would do her any good but

116

being in this huge house alone made Ruby lonelier.

She began to look in the mirror and masturbate right

in front of the mirror. She was so disappointed

because she was successful and beautiful, so why

couldn't she get a man?

The next day at work, Ruby thought about Fred

all day, and at the end of the day he came in her

office without saying a word and gave her a

massage. It felt so good and she couldn't say a

word. He just kept hitting the right spots and Ruby

climaxed sitting right there, but she couldn't say a

word. When he finished, which was right when she

climaxed, he just left as if he knew the job was

done. Later that night, Fred showed up at Ruby's

house. She didn't know how he got away but when he walked in the door, she was in a long satin robe, and she was butt naked underneath. He grabbed her as if she was the only woman in the world. He kissed her passionately, and her whole body exploded. Ruby actually had an orgasm as Fred was kissing her. He led her upstairs to her bedroom and took her robe off. He just stood there and looked at her body as if it was the most beautiful thing in the world. He caressed her body from head to toe. It had been so long that Ruby was actually aching from his touch. He began to kiss her and his lips felt so good next to his that it was just unbelievable. He began to kiss her breast and Ruby began to climax again. Her body was definitely in need of a man and this man was giving her what she wanted. He continued on and she began to respond by undressing him. His body was so hairy that she thought he was half animal, but it was sexy and she wanted him even more. She began to kiss him from head to toe. She started with his sexy lips and then she moved down and gave him oral sex. His whole body shivered and he was so excited, it seemed as if his body turned a flaming red. When Ruby was finished, Fred slid inside of her and it was like she was in heaven. It felt so good and he knew exactly where to put it, which made it even better. They made love for over an hour and they were both exhausted in the end. As she lay in his arms and he stroked her hair, she wished he could stay all night, but she knew he would get up and leave. He began to tell her that he was in love with her and had been for a while. Ruby couldn't move, and for some reason, she believed him. He continued on telling how he had been admiring her from afar and wanted her, but he had to work out some things and wanted to know if she could wait. Ruby was crying and she knew she couldn't wait but it felt so good, so she said yes. He got up and left and Ruby slept better that night than she had slept in years.

The next morning at work, Ruby tried to avoid Fred because she knew she would have that glow.

She didn't see him until later, and he came in her office quietly and gave her one of those killer massages. She couldn't move. He was hitting all the right spots and when he finished and she had climaxed, he walked out and told her he would call her later. Ruby felt so good right then that she cried. She had no idea why she was crying, but she knew it was a good cry. She wasn't sad; in fact, she felt better than she had in years.

When Ruby got home, she lit her entire upstairs with candles and had a relaxing night in her bedroom thinking about Fred. Demi knew something was going on and began to question her Mom. Demi knew she wasn't harassing her anymore so that felt good, but something was different.

"Mom, do you have a man?" she asked.

"What?"

"You just seem to glow these days and you don't hassle me," she said.

"Well, I have to get over whatever this is because I don't want you to be hassle-free," Ruby responded. They laughed and Demi got in the bed with Ruby and told her she wanted to talk. Demi began to tell her about how she felt about this guy and how she wanted to go out on a date. Ruby agreed she could if she talked to him first. So Demi told her she would set it up. Demi and Ruby fell asleep together in Ruby's bed, and that was until the phone rung.

It was 2 am and it was Fred on his cell phone. He told her he had to see her, but he couldn't get away and could she just talk to him for a while. Ruby didn't like the fact that he was at home and she told him she would see him at work. The next morning, Fred was in her office and he threw her on the desk and made passionate love to her right there in her office. Ruby was in shock, but she felt good. Fred was so mysterious, he just walked out, and she didn't see him any more that day. Later on that day, Ruby got an email from Fred that was three pages long. He told her his most intimate feelings for her and how he was miserable without seeing her everyday, all day. He concluded the letter with the fact that he was going to leave his wife and he wanted to meet her in El Paso this weekend, and he was going to make their relationship official. Ruby printed the letter and read it at least ten times. The last two times, she just cried because she couldn't believe it. Believe it or not, she was excited and was waiting for the weekend. Ruby didn't know that Fred was having problems with his wife before they had their affair. She didn't know that he was already planning on leaving his wife but whatever she didn't know, she knew she was happy right now. Demi was going to visit her grandparents for the weekend, so she got in the Lexus and drove to El Paso. Why El Paso, Ruby didn't know, but she smiled all the way there. When she got to the hotel, Fred was already there. He had this glow about him that made Ruby glow. He took her into the hotel's restaurant and ordered coffee.

"It's official, I have left my wife," he said.

"Yeah, but you are not divorced," she said.

"No, not yet, but my lawyer is working on it," he replied.

"I told you I was for real Ruby, I only want you." It was a mutual break-up. He didn't leave his wife for her but when he realized that he wanted Ruby; it helped him to make his decision. He wanted to date her. He wanted her to be his and that the weekend was the start of their relationship. They had a great weekend shopping, relaxing and having great sex. For some reason when Ruby was with Fred, she felt whole and brand new. He had a way of making her feel like the woman she really was.

For the next two years, Fred and Ruby had a great courtship. He got along well with her children, although Damon didn't really like him at first. That was just her son protecting her, but he came around when he saw his mother happy. There were times they had arguments as any couple would but they made it through. Demi graduated from high school and got a scholarship to go to UCLA but she didn't want to be with her brother so she decided to go to Spellman in Atlanta. Ruby didn't like it at first but she had reared a great daughter and she trusted her. So she looked forward to her daughter going off to college and becoming a woman. Ruby and the whole family including Fred took Demi out after the graduation. They were all sitting around talking and laughing when Fred said he had an announcement. He got on one knee and Ruby was astonished.

"I love you and I want you to be my wife," he said. He opened up the ring box and the diamonds were so big, Ruby had to blink her eyes twice.

"I just want to know that for the last couple of years, I have felt good and it's because of you, so I want to make you my wife," he said. Ruby couldn't talk, so she just listened as tears began to roll down her face.

"You make me whole and want to live life again and most importantly, you are real to me and I want to know if you will be my wife?" Ruby couldn't speak, so she just shook her head. Everyone was so happy and they were all cheering especially Damon and Demi. Ruby got up and just began kissing the man she loved and for the first time in a long time, she knew he loved her.

Chapter 7

The next couple of months, Ruby began working on her wedding plans. She was happier than she had ever been in her life. She was out buying for the wedding almost every day. Fred moved in with her, but they were looking to buy another house together. They had not set a date, but they were on their way. For the first time in Ruby's life, a man had been honest with her, and for the first time in her life she really believed this man.

One day after work, Ruby met with one of her best friends, Jane, at Applebee's. They had a couple of drinks, and they were discussing the wedding, and the good old days when Marcus walked in, and he asked Jane could he have a moment. Janie looked at Ruby to get the okay and she went to the bathroom. Ruby couldn't figure out why Marcus was there. She was in love and she had put the past in the past. He seemed so excited to see her. He began telling her he was in town for business, and just happened to see her there. He asked how had life been going for her and she began to tell him. His whole facial expression changed as he sat there and realized that Ruby had changed. She had changed her whole demeanor about life. He also knew that he had no chance to interrupt her life again. As he walked away, Ruby gave a polite smile and thought about all the heartache she had experienced but how she had finally arrived. Marcus knew by her facial expression that she didn't have any room for his lies, so he said it was good to see her and went on by his business. When Jane came back to the table, she laughed at Ruby and told her how proud she was of her.

"I don't know what you said but I know it was the right thing," Jane said. Ruby explained how at this point, she was ready to have the life she always wanted, and they continued to discuss the wedding.

Fred wanted to get married in September, so Ruby had a lot of work to do. She decided on royal blue and silver as their colors. Fred was satisfied with whatever she decided. They decided on having an outdoor wedding in a park. They found the park and began to make arrangements. It was going to be a big wedding because they both had big families and a lot of friends. Time was drawing near, and Ruby began to get nervous. Ruby's mother came to live with them, and Fred leased an apartment. They had found a house, but it seemed as if it would be after the honeymoon before they could move. They even found someone to buy the house they were living in presently. Ruby's mom helped out a lot with all the arrangements and Ruby was glad she was there. They talked a lot about the plans for the wedding, and they seemed to be really close right now. Damon had come home. He had two semesters left, and Ruby was beginning to see the man that she and her mother had reared. He was handsome and he was in the kitchen telling his grandmother about this new girlfriend that was coming to the wedding. Demi was home also. She was still beautiful. She still had the prettiest black hair that any young woman could have.

As the days got closer, Ruby's house began to fill up. She didn't mind, but she didn't see Fred as much. He was busy with his family and getting prepared for the wedding.

The day finally arrived and Ruby was more than ready. She had a beautiful strapless silver dress that was laced with navy roses at the bottom. As she put the dress on, she felt like she had gone through so much hell to finally get to this day, and she was so emotional that tears rolled down her face. She couldn't stop crying because she was so happy. Everything was decorated in blue and silver and the hostess had done a wonderful job. It was a beautiful day, and as Ruby turned the corner to walk down the aisle, she saw Fred. Her father was whispering something to her but all she could see was Fred. He was standing there as if he had been waiting forever, and his chance had finally arrived. He felt good and she could see it on his face. Ruby was more than beautiful; she was extravagant. Her body had a glow about it and she showed it as she walked down the aisle completely focused on her husband to be. When she made it to him, he didn't hesitate, he kissed her on the cheek. The ceremony was short and sweet. Fred and Ruby decided to cite their own vows.

"I knew when I met you, I met my best friend and wife," he said.

"You make me feel like the man I am supposed to be. You give me strength when I am weak and you give me happiness when I am sad. I never thought I could love someone as much as I love you.

135

Today, I dedicate my love and my life to you forever. I promise to you to be the best husband, father, and friend that you could ever have."

Ruby began her vows but she was a mess because she was already crying.

"I love you with all my heart and I am dedicated to giving and showing you all the love that I have to give. You are my best friend and I knew when I met you that you would one day be my husband. You are sweet, kind and loving. I dedicate to you today that I may be your wife, mother to your children, and friend for the rest of my life." Everyone was crying when the minister introduced Fred and Dr. Ruby Grant to the congregation.

The reception was very nice also. It was in one of the facilities at the park. It was decorated so tastefully with silver and blue decorations. After all the pictures were done and Mr. and Mrs. Fred Grant were announced, Ruby was still as radiant as she was when she walked down the aisle. Everyone seemed to just watch her because she was beautiful, and she knew it as she thanked everyone for everything. Fred and Ruby honeymooned in Jamaica and the Bahamas. They enjoyed great food, great sex, and they spent a lot of money, but they were happy. On their last night in the Bahamas, Ruby took a walk on the beach as Fred slept. She was just thanking God that he had brought Fred in her life. She told God that she was forever grateful and that she would be the best wife that she could ever be. Ruby was enjoying the beach when she looked up and saw Fred. They walked and talked and then went back to the hotel room and made love better than they had the whole honeymoon. As Ruby turned over, she had a smile on her face like she had never had in her whole life. She was 45 and had finally reached eternal happiness.

Chapter 8

All good things come to an end, and so Fred and Ruby returned home and tried to go back to normal. She was only teaching one class at the university, and her other time was spent at her beauty shop and her new clothing store. Fred became her legal partner at the clothing store and when he left the university, he came over and did a lot of work at the store. They were having a great time and they were preparing for Damon's graduation from college.

A couple of months had passed and Ruby was missing Damon and Demi a lot but she knew they

139

had their own lives. For the last couple of days, Ruby was feeing really sick and wasn't sure what was wrong, but she really didn't have time to stop to go the doctor. Eventually, Ruby couldn't handle it and made an appointment. After her check-up, the doctor came in and told Ruby the most devastating news she had heard in years. Ruby was eight weeks pregnant. Her whole body shut down, and she called Fred from the car. She remembered Fred saying he wanted a family, but it was the last thing on her mind. Fred finally answered his phone, and she told him that she needed to discuss something with him. He suggested that they meet for dinner and talk about it. They met at their favorite restaurant, Applebee's, and Fred could immediately tell that something was wrong.

"I don't know if you're ready for this," she began.

"Baby, whatever it is, we can work it out," Fred responded.

"I'm pregnant," Ruby said. Fred was so excited that he jumped up and began to scream all over the restaurant that his wife was going to have his baby. Everyone in the restaurant began to laugh and cheer. Ruby couldn't believe it. He was really happy and he told everybody wherever he went. Being pregnant, Ruby really saw how much Fred loved her. He looked at her so different now. Sometimes,

Ruby would wake up and Fred would just be staring at her with a certain type of glare that could not be explained. It was about three months later and Ruby was really showing and they had to go to California to Damon's graduation. Fred and Ruby decided to wait until the graduation to tell Damon and Demi. They were both very surprised that their mother was pregnant, but they were very supportive and caring children. As they sat in the audience at the graduation, Ruby reflected on Damon's accomplishments, and how proud she was of him. He had majored in engineering and had landed a great job in Atlanta, Georgia, making $90,000 a year. He could finally pay for his own BMW. She then thought of the fact that she was starting over. Regardless of how she was glad about Damon graduating, one fact remained in Ruby's head, and that was that she was pregnant and was about to start all over. After the graduation, Ruby and Fred had reserved a banquet hall to have a lavish party. Scott had made a lot of friends, and most of his family was there too. It was a great party. Everyone went back to his or her respective places, and Fred and Ruby went back to their normal activities. Fred was so romantic. He would do some of the most unexpected things at the most unexpected times. He would send flowers or little notes to Ruby at the job, and it would just make her day. What Ruby really like was sometimes when she came home, he would have rose petals from the front door to the bedroom and he would be butt-naked ready for intense sex. Although Ruby felt big and ugly, Fred thought she was more sexier pregnant than she had been before. As Ruby got bigger, the sex wasn't as intense as it was at first.

Around the eight month of pregnancy, Ruby was ready for this baby to come out. They decided not to find out what the baby was going to be beforehand. Ruby decided to take off from work early because she could barely get out of the bed. There was no doubt she was miserable. Fred offered to stay with her but she needed that time alone, so she told him to work until she had the baby. One day as Ruby was going upstairs, she felt a strong pain in the stomach, and she couldn't move. No one was in the house but she had the phone in her hand. She called 911 because she knew this was going to be it. After five hours of intense labor, Fred and Ruby gave birth to a beautiful girl. Fred cried the whole time. He was so excited and happy. They named her Ashley Renée and she looked just like Fred. Fred wouldn't leave Ruby's side holding the baby. They were happy, and the baby was healthy. The doctor had told them they could go home the next day, and they were in the hospital room when a pregnant woman walked in looking at

145

Fred with tears in her eyes. Ruby looked close at her and realized it was Fred's ex-wife.

About the Author

She is the daughter of Elder Dave and Annie Jackson of Camilla, Georgia. She is the mother of two children: Desirae and Byron. She has a bachelor's and master's degree in English from Albany State University. She is currently an English teacher at Albany Technical College in Albany, Georgia.

She has several unpublished manuscripts relating to the struggle of African-American women and African Americans in the south, but decided to write about love, which is also a struggle for African-

American women. She has edited several novels for publication and has worked for newspapers as a copy editor and as a reporter.